## PRAISE FOR *WALKING & STEALING*

"Since the late 90s, Stephen Cain has stayed in the game to drive the line with work marked by his commitment to the local, intertextual, and communal. *Walking and Stealing* sees Cain at his most raucous. These poems are fully loaded—they crack, cut, dive, and play double. With a poetics steeped in devotion to the unorthodox, Cain proves himself again to be one of Canada's foremost avant-gardists who continues to expand the field."

—Eric Schmaltz, author of *Surfaces* and *Borderblur Poetics*

"Equal parts logophilic love song and searing post-punk lament, Stephen Cain's *Walking and Stealing* is a Molotov cocktail for the city dweller's soul. With playful constraints and sprawling seriality, Cain takes us on psychogeographic drifts and dérives, sends us spinning through allusive urban thickets, and leads us on unapologetic intertextual joyrides through a city and a world on fire. This sauntering tome is whip-smart and shady AF—a semiotic feast at every turn."

—Kate Siklosi, author of *Selvage*

## PRAISE FOR *FALSE FRIENDS*

"Stephen Cain offers hifalutin (and low) games, lots of play on and
with various 'friends' in literature & art, and a decisive retort to
the personal lyric."

—Douglas Barbour

"Much great poetry requires a negotiation of new worlds, an
assessment of innovative structures, or a willingness to abandon
all predeterminations. *False Friends* performs these criteria
through total upheaval—a rewiring of readers' brains—leaving in
its wake both liberation and confusion."

—*Broken Pencil*

"In *False Friends*, Cain revels in a play of sound and meaning,
bouncing his narrative as a pinball across the field of language."

—rob mclennan's blog

"A dense, inventive book [that]...traffics heavily in alliteration and
meaty-sound combinations."

—*Winnipeg Free Press*

# WALKING & STEALING

## STEPHEN CAIN

WALKING &

Book*hug Press
Toronto 2024

# STEALING

## STEPHEN CAIN

Library and Archives Canada Cataloguing in Publication

Title: Walking and stealing / Stephen Cain.
Names: Cain, Stephen, 1970– author.
Identifiers: Canadiana (print) 20240340965 | Canadiana (ebook) 20240345509
    ISBN 9781771669108 (softcover)
    ISBN 9781771669191 (EPUB)
Subjects: LCGFT: Poetry.
Classification: LCC PS8555.A4624 W35 2024 | DDC C811/.6—dc23

The production of this book was made possible through the generous assistance
of the Canada Council for the Arts and the Ontario Arts Council. Book*hug Press
also acknowledges the support of the Government of Canada through the Canada
Book Fund and the Government of Ontario through the Ontario Book Publishing
Tax Credit and the Ontario Book Fund.

Book*hug Press acknowledges that the land on which we operate is the
traditional territory of many nations, including the Mississaugas of the Credit, the
Anishnabeg, the Chippewa, the Haudenosaunee, and the Wendat peoples. We
recognize the enduring presence of many diverse First Nations, Inuit, and Métis
peoples, and are grateful for the opportunity to meet and work on this territory.

# Book*hug Press

*For Cy*

We shall build our city backwards from each baseline
    extending like a square ray from each distance—you from
    the first-base line, you from behind second baseman,
    you from behind the short stop, you from the third-baseline.
We shall clear the trees back, the lumber of our pasts and
    futures back, because we are on a diamond, because it is our
    diamond

**Jack Spicer**


some planet that loves not cider hath conspired against me

**Thomas Nashe**

# CONTENTS

# WALKING & STEALING

# 1. Christie Pits (2017/05/11)

Freed weed
Pits the chill
White soundmark
Studio 54 font
Between the screens
L bows

A less talented donut
Blood on the bench
Triffid systems
Go blonde
Ambit notion
Scramble timeblind

Switch hats
Come on Columbia
Remember your feet
Silly man new pretence

A Saran Wrap psychopath
Another seductive sadist
Mule-minded
Burro wrath
Donne's deathmask

First thought worst thought
Pressure remains
Dig out the k-hole
Hey naught naughty

Aeolian HAARP
Aerial dismay
A Cylon skyline
Silurian sunset
Wrist wounds
Isometric icing
Load up early

Those 222s
Blues plaint

Pen is cold
Phallic that
Shorter by par

Movement moments
Numbered plays

## 2. Christie Pits (2017/05/12)

Death slips
Peristalsis panic
Glop dog
From the master's throat

Appropriative response
Think in synonyms
Settler dissimilitude
Slime always surfaces
Leper City Landlords

Emotional miscue
Negative as charged

Knot knavery
Havoc herald
Galactic snafu

That's the pitch
Perfect perfidy
Unearned erring
Complicated or kinder
Morgellon music
Threnody park

Greetings from Grimm
Wolf missal
Hymnals for hymens
Grand slam guignol

Shiva shakes
Hanuman howls
Pantheon pillage
Mining myths

Back to racists
Billy-bat bragging
To make scarce & scared
Break the Fourth Estate gates

Our own owed

## 3. Stan Wadlow Park (2017/05/13)

Instant idyllic
Graffitigram grin
It's an orange
Tropicalia trumps Tims
Cannibal lector
A civil split
Roadwar Two

Badnews bares
Take the field
Formerly known

Colour my transfer
Complete catharsis
   inconceivable
A good park to start
Respark the dark

Heart-marked head cold
A cat with nine lies
Pussy new what's
Novel not much
Close Shavian moral play
Done John time in Hell

A game changer
Salt & pepper chaser
Gunsmoke sky
No augury under
   demagoguery
Zodiac ozone

Stopping for souvlaki
Czech point gnarly
Barley horn plenty
Likes lend lustre
Thumb the corner
What a fine toy am I

A reign delay
Rainbow warning
Gotta use aluminum
   somewhere
Enlightenment strikes

Tracing the trochees
Keeping the rhythm method
Acting in concordance
With or Withnail you
Nice pegs shame about the
   grace

A mutiny on boundaries

## 4. Christie Pits (2017/05/26)

Treecide

Leeside

Scarecrow stump

Bounded in a newt's hell

Fling in a fidelis space

Never home coming

Past favourite park

Don't kiss

Sharing's sick

Porcupine dentata

Invigilate the Inferno

Commodious circumstance

Cue skirt

Firecracker cap

A fame thrower

A lightning dolt

A compact catcher

Dig in dyke

Warm up for wormfood

The evil head

God eye

Smoke & swagger

Gumshoe bubble bounce

Stupid haiku

Sight supremacy

Jinx mix

Drink venue

The best pitched

Plans of dice & zen

## 5. Concord Regional Park (2017/06/02)

Childmoon coldsweat
With best lines behind
Tourniquet tie off
KC at last

Speed thrills
Three on a dime
Not scorched keeping
Hellion hardball
Here comes the light

Zukofsky shorthand
Double A divining
Fighting through the *Cantos*

A new picture
The ditch of poetry
Ooh la la lewd bard
British Knight stomped down

Local habits
Br'er burns
Werewolf love
Fullmoon freebase
All your taste is mine

The dactylic clap
Anapests are the champions

Smoke blanket
Sweet sheets
A snake in the ass

Ground covered

## 6. Christie Pits (2017/06/09)

It reigns; it pores
Glory gallows Judas-bait
Jonesing for jiu-jitsu
Red nail crucifuck

Bloodied by Bunnyhug &
   Ballyhoo
Echoes Layla on your knees
Pitch perfect, reverse is true

Brewing up bedbugs
Injury phone
Emoji rescue
Paint it lacks

Blitz league
Storm fronting
Love enough rough
Alls in, coming frown

Broken plate
Palate able
So thin scary vice
An economy of need
Withhold the middle
Laughter expense

Berth Day Buoys
A Diet Coke in Warsaw
Joy Divisible
Unknown Measures

Stay in the game
Lectured by a hipster
Millennial pretension
Tricky woo me
A poem a day in play

Visualization Griffin lore
A pretty prize for poesy
Follow the hermit
Crabwise pounds
Gunshot gifts to girlfriends
& still the fame remains

An Egyptian blue jay
Whiskey Jack MacEwen
Hiawatha élan lost in the fens
Swampsick miasma
Gaslighting the nightingale

Call blue a code bruise
The Miller's Tale of tail
Golden flowers flow

Warm bottled walker
Johnny come early
Not me meme
Charitably laid in the mind

The turn of the bride

## 7. Iroquois Park (2017/06/16)

Garden parties
Weed & wilding
That's right, mascara snake
A walking eyebrow
Spiderwebs in my mailbox
Spiderbots in my inbox

Leprechaun legerdemain
Jeffery of the Jungle
Gives currant cede
High doltage
Face to pace the random
    tilling

Bit by something
Tickle me emo
The Necessary Angle
Too tenuous to terminate
A truth ache
Denial surgery

Too few to use
A June buggy
Gem eye double cited
You are a vaper fail

A one run stalking
Moss Park story
Still as a stone
Gathering gallants
Six rolls to one

Grade-school girlfriends
    at the game
Early barter
Italian ingénue
Fortunata Donna
All I can say in anguish

Foray zeal
Echoes of Ottawa
By water or by ward
A spell caste
Something germane
Or gamine

Curtain chewer or pillow biter
Widespread wallpaper
Painting with DNA
Prime scene instigation

## 8. Milliken Mills Park (2017/06/20)

Savage vegetarian
Vicious vegan
The fascism of foodies
Alcohol is my yoga

Superman 'splaining
The Batman's a robber
& Star Boy's a psycho
Pet names for pervs

Hardball on the Heath
Leary prospects penned
Wanton flyballs to boys
Such gods abscond

4:48 metempsychosis
Another body hovers
Bedroom bedlam
Halfway to Dreamtime
Songline sorrow

A coming honeymoon
Mustard bath meltdown
Six seasons of celibacy
Dry white whine
Know your signs

Every crew's a 42
Dark cloud gardening
Allow some levity
Eerie Irie
A Rasta in passim

She should have been a sun
Another tedious pun
Oxyrhynchus fish
Or castrating bitch
Latent in the legend

Osiris & Orpheus
St. Joseph's balls
Bruised & blued
Picabia knew the score
Drew the Virgin as a whore

A puck jock pretender
Ultimate asshole
Laissez-faire Frisbee fuck
Rosedale faux Romeo
Scion scum with trust fund

## 9. Christie Pits (2017/06/24)

I

All I haunt is you
A cuckold made Christ
& that's my middle name

How to disappear,
   incompletely
You can go crazy fucking these
   ghosts
Ectoplasmic orgasms
Marks of spectres

The dog's got a death wish
String Thanatos
Chocolate lag
Mushroom thaumaturgy

Return to Cage
The elephant in the gloom

Saying, "miss it, miss it"
Grounds for ejection
Disputing a call
Unknown numbers
Suddenly remembered
Lines driven
Futon fumbles
Heavy debting

Forced fields
Protective verse
Steve's Olson
Maximus: six million hollering
   men
Out of the needy, none

Hard & level
Heading for extinction
Much talk of telos
Anthropocene means
Too many men at the table
Greenhouse gassing
Lights out for the predatory

One law for the LAN & the
  AUX is oppression
Blakelite luminescence
Pretty nuclear
Vaguely Viriconium
Mac Low's lighthouse warning
See stones & bones
Wreck Beach beckoning
A missed inopportunity
Venus visions
A balm belle

Yakety Sex
Benny Hill innuendo
A closet trauma
Bedroom scars
Farcical fantasies
A quartet of quislings
Of a spawning satyr
Let alone a liar

Take a break Thackeray
All vanity's fair
Love & more
Brothers in harm
Doves on a battlefield
& no bards sang

Barely loitering
A night in arms
A prick in a pith helmet
Colonizing home bodies
Soap bubble seduction
In a blink of snow
Ere indie disaster

Fireball's my wit's key
Think of choice
Me & my whine
Liver laughter; renal rictus
Bilious imbibing
Potted philosophy
Socrates was a souse

II

Legs in the air
Vultures flying up above
Another useless weekend
Killed in dub

Living in stereo
Moving in mono
Two-channel interference
Quadrophobia

Tough luck, keep pitching
An awe patrol
Pound's puppies in Pisa
A salad for centurions
Daily decimation

Poor Paddy, crying
The pour mouth
A little liquid dig
Piss on me, I'm Irish
Erin's monotheism
Snivilization discontent

A base in the sun
Eyeballing Africa
Mussolini undertow
Ubu in Ethiopia

You too, Darling Nikki
Fears & tears
Lolita station
Wishful drinking
Exhausting triskaidekaphobia
Who by the pyre?

Seasoned stories
Wanted the shrimp plated
Some seafood on the side

Like to write a backwards K
But the KKK in this place
Is no striking sign
Anti-Semitism recycled
Heidegger's hubris
Bruno burns

Tracking tribbles & triffids
Imaginary invertebrates
Newton's nonsense
Patageography
Push past the pornographic
    perspective
Libidinal landscape

Barefoot in the dark
Blinded by a blonde
Discus dryad
The sylphs of Scarborough

Waiting for the withdrawal
Homer turns cyclopedian
Diderot dictates
Danton's malfunction

## 10. Howard Talbot Park (2017/06/29)

Grand Theft Auto
In the Greater Toronto Area
Crime & the city's pollution
Six belles of mine
An attempt at exhausting
   a face

We split after Ashbery
Lyrics in a vending machine
Sonnet cigarettes
Cold poultry pastoral

Taking it all black
Basic burnouts
Aerosol arsenal
Bug bombs for Pasadena
Kali education

Drama dreams
Anxiety ordered
Sarah Kane, my main
Liner note quotes

Toronto tropical
Weathering the scorn
August announced early
Calendar conjunction crisis
Sidereal sickness
#throwupthursday
Star dross lovers

What's the lore?
At the bottom of the legend
Troll another monster in
   that mode

Pun aground

Just leave it up there
A signal scores too
Ladies to the left
Gents GOP stopped

A perfect encirclement
Rheostatic interference
Broken, local, mean
A clique for the curious

Keeping it tight
Hemingway smile
Papa Doc's rages

Abhor Alberta

A Calgarian cowpuncher

Creative writing comportment

Let lies lie

A pale pink pearl

Heathrow heartache

A word traveller

Fortune flies exec

Flay the friendly eyes

Concussion collusion

An imaginary invalid

Perversely persistent

Sympathy for the left bro

Second favourite field

A fear of living dangerously

The prints of exile

The rainbow succession

## 11. Christie Pits (2017/06/30)

& was this gruesome place
   builded here
On Eaton's playgrounds
   green?

Albion's Angel at the corner of
   Kipling
Enitharmon in Etobicoke
Snakes of the North
Lost in Mississauga
Rattled
      "fall down dead"

A tag through the traffic:
"bp was here"
   Haunts these lines
   Walks those lanes
   A lone punman

Accidental, not disappeared
Smoke, not light
I had not thought debt had
   undone so many
Surreal City

I see the lich of Layton at
   Langstaff
Yoked to York
Musing upon Montreality

Inching along the shore
   of Iroquois
Davenport where Spadina
   splits
Secedes from the Annex
Jane's Jacobin rebellion
The Republic of Rathnelly
Toronto, the hood

Robin Whiskeyjack
Sherwood Forest Hill
Hijack the Skywalk
Storm the Dome
The Bastille of baseball

Here's Hawksmoor in
   Hogtown
Where Schafer synchronizes
   with Sinclair
The minotaur at midtown
Daedalus devises delirium
Cloverleaf roundabout railpath
Backlane historians

Articulate the known-lines
Map the Masonic
Toronto Chthonic

Get him on the rundown
Pick off the precocious
They eventually hoist
    themselves
Gallows for goofs

Fighting words, a panopticon
    punchout
Rough trades for the Bay
    Street boys
The Buddha of Mount Baldy
A koan by Cohen
Booze blues
Raincoat shuffle
An impersonation for introverts

Some grass on the hill

Christie chronic
*Le Dejeuner sur l'herbe*
Without the naked nymphs

Foxes think fondly of fawns
Coltish capering
Chickenhawk dawn patrol

It is resolved by walking

If I had a Nietzsche hammer
Remember your whip
    pussyboy
Rub it with bones

Skinny begs for all
Half asleep in fog
    panjandrums
Another roadside contraption
Long weekend lassitude
Guarded Godard

## 12. McGregor Park (2017/07/05)

The avant-garde always turns
   occult
A tarot card writing

Chemical gnosis
Drinking my way toward
   Jerusalem

Just here for the green tea
Bubble battles, the toil of
   troubles

Worker on a rig, wrecking
   *The Warriors*
"Can you dig dug it?"

A panoramic playground
Pixilated

## 13. Christie Pits (2017/07/21)

Atrocious anniversaries
   approach
Wicked ways & plays
At bay in the fields of the Ford

The tall men of Toronto
Crass of the titans
Kirby dot demolition

Line it up—I'll hate it
Fabulous dunderheads of
   Downsview
Yorked again

Enjoy life in the fast lane
This queer Utopia
You're never alone with a
   phone

Seriously amiss
Blake's spiders have six legs
Sinister sonneteer
Letters from my left hand

Begs for days
Traced with an aardvark
   tongue
Knocking them out with those
   American eyes

Back in the swing
Like a friendly Fragonard
   game
Erotic poetics
Dr. Williams recommends

Ballard's blueprints of Babylon
"I am Zion man"
A teapot of gin
A genius in the bottle

Skull cheese
Ahead by a sentry
Cover your mouth when you
   scoff

Sort out your sympathies
Divide up the devils
Detail your denials
Roll or atone

*The Third Man*

In tights I see tonight
Forgot my witch's wand
New batteries for the battle
Diamonds & perils

Little bomb, who made thee?
That *Tiger Beat* glow
Bikini breach
Atoll to tell

## 14. Christie Pits (2017/07/22)

An acephalic mermaid
The Situationists & Surrealists
At the Sorbonne

Water punked squirt fun
Plug & play
Rue the consequences
Mix & go

Did Jekyll kill Hyde or did I?

Read to be
Kiss & slide
This place of disgrace
A Christmas tree skyline

My most American moment
The invention of seriality
Poems & killers

Focus on the foundation
Modes of militarism
Been caught feeling
Once, when alive

Pain's addiction
Peri-poetic parallel
Farewell to the paperback
    prince

Spittle field hill work
I see something white
Can't I spy your own eye
Find My ePode

Up the middle
Stuck in the conjunction
Triangulate your desire
Time is called

It's not yours
Set the fee
Return on the rebound
Cheque your privilege

Balance the fouls
Bane ball blame
Covenant of co-parents
Pit bull pretty
Slide to a stop

Google car gangland
The laddie in red
Electric blue review
A dance you can't forget

Wash away the singe of
    the world
Kyrie liaison
Know enough Latin to
    recognize the lash

## 15. Lampman Lane Park, Barrie (2017/07/29)

I

Poets see it coming
Canaries of the code minds
Power will fail; branches
   will fall
Ozone blondes
A party with no children

Venus de Milo in a beret
Ran over a dogwood
Orchestral voices
A B+ kiss of death

Emit timE
Letters never sent
Messages in the bread mould
An odd number for an
   exorcism

The crush bleeds through
   the black
Everything echoes
A neurotic dog
Or glamorous economists

Fill your profane thanks
Outside the store

Given a licence to chill
We break bonds
Shakened by her stirring

Lampman's longing
Sue run ruin
Singing frogs stuffed in a
   bottle

March here
Metric measures
Stand & deliberate

Cottaging British country style
A slide between the sheaves
Miss Muffet's way

Son on the mound
Lowing calls
A dodge whistle
Own the sound

Barrie's big
Namesake noted
What's a philippic for
If you can't satirize the
   disguise?

We've got eyes
An R in the sky
Brie among the blue
Too much cheese

A Friday the 13th fracture
Waiting for the raptor
Overused views
Return of the reforgotten

A new picture
Exhibition embryo
Tyranto Tyranna
Potato potatoe

Pouty horsemouth
Bee-stung quips
Quarter-sleeve inking
Rockstar drinking

Running out of seams
A Swiftian tailor
Sartor restart us
Bring it all honed

## II (Christie Pits, 5 pm)

Another fink coming
TAZ deviltry
Buggers at Bey
All gone wrong in the Tong

Hit on at the Rhino
Gym Rat King
Aurora boredom
Northern blights

Charge into the love
Electric morning come

The buzz of the blades of
    grass

The mutterings of matter
Atomic asshole, Frankly
Anus horribilis
An alpha male wannabe

The slaughter of the inner
    sense

Designated drives
Tim foolery
Use it or I will scry

Cancelled crooks
I don't want to follow a
    hyperlink
I want the hyperlink to follow
    me

Bell the Sabbath in
No Sunday stopping
The excommunication that
    proves the tool

Golden boy of Winnipeg
As mean & as male as Manson
A Guy Maddin gal
Drinking your own Kool-Aid

Scramble for Africville
The unbearable whiteness of
    Gleeing
Use Bowering as a battery
Ordinary infernal machinery

Enjoys muddying the
    daughters
The pop of patriarchy
Call the ball: "Yo La Tangle"

Games in progress
Count the scores
Sick one

Made a little music
*Nacht Kleine*
Boxing with the sun
Repeat velocity

Dillinger opaque plan
Guns of Neverland
Brixton or Bracebridge
Beware rented waterfronts

A smug seduction
Smash that smile

## 16. Christie Pits (2017/08/11)

After us the Savage Mob
The ghosts of Jarry park
Answer, a bad time to be Bloor

Curates egg on
Parts the whole
Uncles claim: no depression
Both bad at that

OK, blue days
Let's Paxil

Thrown, like a girl
Collaging for conclusions
Lost all the lines on arising

Animals don't exaggerate
   illness
A flippant dolphin
Or cynical cetacean

Whale tale wonderment
Job over Jonah
My trophy knife
Cuts like a life

Calling Dr. Caligari
Lost in the cabinet shuffle
An expressionist academic
No one needs a dealer
After they've scored

Who wants Guam?
Trident miss kills
Mutual Assured Deduction
Blink first, last blink

Fires of Fukushima
Coals of Chernobyl
Isotope tropes
Vehicles subject to Tenor

The Day the Earth Stood Ill
Klaatu's kindness
No palliative against POTUS

Table's set
My brunch with Breton
Andre's dinner of soluble fish
Inquisitive corpse charade

Elevators to Toronto
Hell's escalation
Darkness made risible
Paradise costs

My schoolboy scholarship
Poseur poetry
A bad lecher stripped bare
By his eyes even

## 17. Stan Wadlow Park (2017/08/12)

I

An extinguishing dimension
Eggheads in the outfield
Clear the dreck
Smoke in bed

A rosined labia
Phallic puppet-play
Smile like you're sappy
When Irish ties are lying

Meth means death
Let's all do the nuclear
Hang the Bee Gees
No need for Polaroids anymore

Do not fuck with Adolf Wölfli
Do not even rattle your ice
Mingus might get mad

Enola alone
A gay Yaga
Historical alignments
Month-to-month recitation

Burnish the schoolhouse bricks
People in glass blouses
Can I get a yellow card?
Amen alcoholics

Waiting on an umpire's decree
Start with a walk
A crawling king makes
Aggressive erotic overtures

An old cowboy mouth
Gumming gunslinger
Dorn adjourned
A lousy legendary lyric

Shepard lost, sheep at play
Goaty boys' barnyard
   bedroom

Still many sheaves
Even needs ice

Dude sucking his dentures
Publisher put out to pasture
Sinclair Lewis typing tutor
Capote capo

Stretching the shutdown
Bleed the fifth

II

Map the Moores
Lede line locations
Also Etrog the obelisks
Opposing the ovarian objects

Short & sequestered in
   Scarborough
No more sinister than Sarnia
Oshawa obeisance
Adolescent anxiety
   accumulators
Score on the fly
Beach bleacher bingo
Blanket the yield

Walking & stealing

# INTENTIONAL WALKS

**1.**

In Ireland Now that Spring
As green as given

Lapidary Livias leak lime

Sinn Fein signage
Toilets fir gents

The invention of hospitality
The first hurdle

A language without cognates

Fáilte again
Fáilte better

**2.**

St. Nicotine
Authentic ammo

Loot from the Hip
The Kingston brio

Vulgar boatmen
Beyond the bail

Depressing post-midnight button fly

**3.**

Loving the Nazis to own the Commies
A Society for a Better Sarnia

Paratactic pals
Cut up or shut up

**4.**

"I'd rather burn in Canada"
Anglo Empire Pink

A swig & a miss

**5.**

Risible party lies
Affirm infinity

Since language points to
But never touches

**6.**

Silence from the suburbs
Buried among cows & cars

I'm with Cupid

A streetcar Orpheus
A subway Eurydice

**7.**

A lot of preamble
For not much payoff

Propriety is thrift

No honorifics on a tombstone

**8.**

In permanent retrograde
"Decipher this whiteness"

Not pretty but pouty

Anger is an allergy

**9.**

More Songs About Feist
Stay in your own vein

Polis is police

**10.**

*The Interpretation of Memes*
Little lamb, who ate thee?

**11.**

A competent poet

Held at gunpoint by Calliope
Not amused

**12.**

Not much hope in that chest

Write for free
To save your CV

Don't call the fax machine

**13.**

The Buddha's dada
That's King Suddhodana to you

Confucius had some cash

Too old to skate
But the Vans look great

**14.**

Presidential paranoia
Means mitigate against megalomania:
Killing an Ahab

White wails

**15.**

Know I like a little gnocchi
Ladies Love Cool Duchamp

Chessboard bros
Sarcastic mannequins

The Fountain overflows
Too ursine in the cubicle

**16.**

"Word up [up up] it's the code word"
Sucker rhymesters
Radio limbo

Instagram lyricism
They think they're fly

Makeup melts
Around Emma B's eyes

**17.**

*Twerking to the Oldies*
In a *Star Wars* story without light sabres

Semi-psychedelic screaming ids
You & your sloppy daughter

Sad, like a siren
Depressed desires

**18.**

Rave on reminisces
Nostalgia for Jungle

2-steps from the middle ages
Pigs of the apocalypse
Feral, or otherwise

Orcas & Kraken
Aquatic avatars of our extinction

**19.**

Dial M for *The Martyrology*
Get thee to a gunnery

Sparks fly from every insurrection

Widowmaker weather

**20.**

Woodworm writing
Critter cryptography

Purloined, like Poe
Live by the letter

**21.**

Can't be a fireman
If you have a headdress on your vest

**22.**

Ska is best over breakfast

Playing Erasure in utero
Will make the baby gay

Unicorns & rainbows
Dora & Boots

But the backpack is a girl

**23.**

*Internet's Down: A Journal of Poetry*

**24.**

Not only bad, but irritating
Also ubiquitous

Partisan politics
Twitter tweaking

Bread & circuits

**25.**

Pretty, but crazy
Crazy, but pretty

*Sintentional Walks*

**26.**

Fascists have failsons
A 12-step pogrom

*And he disrespected the Wu-Tang Clan*

Hal Hartley made me buy smokes
Dangerous, but sincere

**27.**

Sucks, like Achilles in his tent

The racist bones in my body:
I'm trying to break them

**28.**

Stressed & depressed
A risky mouth

It's a wounderful life

**29.**

Trained, like a seal

Carmelite rifles
You can't kill Kundera

*The Book of Rapture & Regretting*

Born under the sign of Carnival

**30.**

A wish doctor
A kiss witch

A slowjob
A sliptease

**31.**

Before the Greenbelt comes the Grimebelt

TTC Gnostics

Golf, or flog

**32.**

Brossard loves Béliveau
Hockey at the Hotel Clarendon

Ecriture over icing
Hail the heroine

**33.**

Surely gaucheness must follow
All the ways of their lies

Some psalms for balms

**34.**

Will read for wine

**35.**

Pablo Picasso was called an asshole

All the time

**36.**

It's the velvet trust
That really drives you sane

Let's do the crime thwart again

**37.**

So sew that S on your chest

Given/taken
Like the cop that gets the apple

A luau for pigs
Turn the tables on totalitarianism

**38.**

A first edition
Silver foxing on the side

Bibliographic babes
Or asexual archivists

Those lines I wrote
By rote

Salacious citations

**39.**

To make skateboards respectable again

Which bees were these?
Knife fights of the near future

Drover Breach

Bovine breakthroughs

**40.**

All armies are ignorant
Weary of redoing poetry wars

Your customers are also your competitors

**41.**

Day of the Dead desires
Frida decisions

Phantastical like Fantômas
Aggressive transgressive

Vestment venery
Pretty boy penury

History retreats upon itself

**42.**

Not done with that narrative

Goethe's gonads
Old man onanism

Stockings still cause sadness

Best leave it to Beckett

**43.**

Mother slay I

Slapped for playing with snatches

Anti-Electra on the Lost Plateau

Tarzan's textbooks

Crusoe & other colonial assholes

**44.**

*How to Make Enemies*
  *& Alienate People*

Write poetry

Viva lost wages

**45.**

Stalker or psychogeographer
Both involve the Zone

Andrei Apollinaire

Benjamin the bridesmaid

**46.**

All style & no story

No meaning, where none intended

**47.**

Old houses make weird noises

Cruel Britannia
Britannia waives the rules

Brexit gambit

To be Bartleby

**48.**

In tide pools of the Tide pod generation

Bot says wot?

Exit, stage cleft

**49.**

The ouroboros factory

Twitter verse, not the Twitterverse
"They came from insta-space"

My memewars begin at berth

**50.**

Dufferin autocorrects
To Suffering

51.

Isn't she petty in pink?

The thrift shop aesthetic

Charity stocks & socks
Find me at the salvage store

Lost & profound

**52.**

Etobicoke after dark

An American Juggalo

Tying one on

Go fucking knots!

**53.**

A fist full of proverbs
For a few followers more

Indecisions cause divisions

**54.**

Eel-eyed mantras

Drive fast:
Live fish!

**55.**

* Exclaiming the question
The only marks to use

Corollary colons

**56.**

Herr Majesty's a pretty nice peril
But she doesn't have a lot of plays

Munich Eunuch

Innocent vicars

**57.**

In a decade where

THIS IS PARADISE

Is displaced by

YOU'VE CHANGED

**58.**

Ok grammar grandma

**59.**

Skinhead mailmen
Tattooed typists

Gendered telecommunication

Fly translove airways

**60.**

Pushing a moose up a ramp

A noose for the newbie

I saw a movie once

**61.**

Making shins sexy again

Soccer succor

But, Nietzsche on the Beach
Nietzsche on the Beach
Nietzsche & Me

**62.**

Derrida's hedgehog
Curling upon itself

Wind in the billows

Failing to Byzantium

**63.**

Scent of cyprine
Reminiscent musk

Roots & roots

**64.**

The sophistry of centrists
Absolut dogma

**65.**

Paging Robert Duncan

Elaborate & arbitrary

Believe in Breatharians

**66.**

Orphaned by Australia

Ecologists are the new arsonists

When 2 + 2 = jive

**67.**

An OK KO in TO

Oroonoko flows

A Behn in the river

**68.**

The first-born unicorns
Alberta springs, an advantage

A seemless transition

The indecision is final

**69.**

Kill switch operation

Walks like a dead plan

Willful paradox or deliberate dilemma

**70.**

The Dance of the Seven Dishrags

Beard maintenance in the age of the anthropocene

My resting crazy face

Grieving & writing

**71.**

S.C.E.X.
Spells Perspex
That's Plexiglas to you

CCTV ubiquity
The insurrection involuntarily televised

**72.**

Playground psychopaths
Where the phallus is inscribed
Underneath the slide

**73.**

Peter as an animal
Stuffed mammals

A tasteful presentation
A plate full of intention

**74.**

Incest enmeshes   .
Meant metaphorically

Take Toronto
Please

**75.**

Ha ha
Said through a nose of snow

That's Mr. Assface to you

Bottomed, like a baboon

**76.**

Ducks, limited

**77.**

I tip my fat to you
My dad bode

An immense grease

Grey for daze

The Sontag Syndrome

**78.**

A maxim on a barn door
Proverbial farmyard

Why we go to zoos

A shirt cited solution

**79.**

Embarrassing epaulettes
The excrescence that hangs from your shoulder

To you, like an aero

**80.**

The dead pigeon poem
Why CanLit is shit

Alongside imperialism
Yty whining

YYZ caprice

**81.**

Bake a cake
According to Skeat

Holye's hobbies
Create Robert's rues

**82.**

A Barbie—or Barthes—Doll
Recites, *myth is hard*

*Let's go shopping*
For a new math for a modern age

Opprobrium, or otherwise
Otiose offering

**83.**

Ubiquitous Ubu tattoos
That's evol to you

Blues bruise

**84.**

& there you are
Looking at the camera, directly

& smiling FFS

**85.**

Your mechanical arresting heart
Beating, like a cop

A Caucasian jerk circle

**86.**

Manic Mussorgsky
Or rioting for Rights

Springs Arab or maple

Always signifies a sacrifice

Russian maestros

Where Putin putts Puccini

**87.**

Attrition by a thousand
Nicks & nets

A bath chair for Brooklyn

Wheeling & reeling

Fiddling while the poem burns

**88.**

Part of your cycle of fiends

Octopus earrings
Oligarch earnings

Double O venom

Snakes & satyrs

**89.**

Sometimes chutes
Eats reads & leaves

Papyrus pays *pukka*

Letterpress poets

Cash on the fail

**90.**

Another pleasant rally sundry
Here the static cynic brand

Liquid paper promises

**91.**

I before thee
Except after cede

**92.**

Aesthetic resistance
Or praising plagiarism

Subversive pleasure
Sucking on s'words
Which cause s'laughter

**93.**

Mexican maxims:
We don't need no stinking adages

**94.**

When whales & dolphins walked on land

A Rochefoucauld hotel

Will outlast us

**95.**

Barrio speed wagon

Trujillo teleologic

Total Toto

Yunior Gone Wilde

**96.**

Stealing signs ain't cheating
Baby Buddha boundaries

Zero to three philosophy

Origins & Oreos

**97.**

Too curmudgeonly for company
Each section ends in self-excoriation

My louche self

**98.**

The opposite of diversity is not unity

## 99.

Old lines, in new battles

## April 25/2019 – Feb. 20/2020

1. South Baggot at Grand Canal to Phoenix Park, Dublin
2. Sheppard & Jane to Sentinel & Finch
3. Queen & Woodbine to Waverley
4. Bloor & Dorval to Bloor & Keele
5. Pacific & Dundas to Dundas & Glenlake
6. Eglinton & Yonge to Eglinton & Bayview
7. Dundas West Station to York University
8. Bloor & Dundas to Roncesvalles & Howard Park
9. Queen & Roncesvalles to Roncesvalles & Marion
10. Keele & Bloor to Dundas & Bloor
11. Sentinel & Sheppard to Sentinel & Finch
12. Eglinton & Yonge to Yonge & Erskine
13. Bloor & Runnymede to Bloor & Windermere
14. Dorval & Edna to Dorval & Chelsea
15. College & Clinton to Clinton & Henderson
16. Jane & Finch to Jane & Sheppard
17. Roncesvalles & Grenadier
19. Dundas approaching Dupont
20. Bloor & Ossington to Bloor & Dufferin
21. Iroquois Park, Whitby
22. College & Lippincott to College & Bathurst
23. 80 Edna Ave.
24. Atkinson Rd. to Pond Rd.
25. Bloor & Dundas to Dundas & Roncesvalles
26. Jane & Bloor to Runnymede & Bloor
27. Yorkdale Station to Wilson Station
28. Queen & Lansdowne to Queen & Roncesvalles
29. Stockyards to Dundas & Keele

30. Jane & Steeles to Steeles & Keele
31. Ontario St. to Lake St., St. Catharines
32. High Park loop
33. Ellis Ave. to Runnymede
34. College & Clinton to College & Shaw
35. Lakeshore & 22nd St.
36. Roncesvalles & Garden to Dundas & Bloor
37. Bloor & Indian Grove to Bloor & Dorval
38. York Blvd. to Ian MacDonald Blvd.
39. Bloor & Bedford to Bedford & Prince Arthur
40. Bloor & Bathurst to Bloor & Christie
41. Weston & Highway 7 to Highway 7 & Pine Valley Dr.
42. Bloor & St. George to Harbord & St. George
43. Dundas & Ossington to Ossington & Dufferin
44. Dupont & Dufferin to Dufferin & Geary
45. Dufferin & York University Busway to Murray Ross
46. Eglinton & Yonge to Eglinton Park
47. Glenlake & Keele to Glenlake & High Park Ave.
48. Humberside & Keele to Humberside & Quebec
49. Queen & Sorauren to Queen & Dunn
50. Dufferin & Bloor to Bloor & Margueretta
51. Bloor & Lansdowne to Bloor & Dundas
52. Queensway & Royal York to Queensway & Islington
53. Jane & Annette to Jane & Bloor
54. Annette & Pacific to Annette & Keele
55. Eglinton & Dixie to Eglinton & Tomken
56. Simcoe to Rossland, Oshawa
57. Queen & Spadina to Queen & Bathurst
58. Annette St. Library
59. Bloor & Palmerston to Bloor & Christie

60. Dundas & Royal York to Dundas & Scarlett
61. Yonge & Carlton to Carlton & Church
62. Annette Community Centre
63. Bloor & Ossington to Bloor & Dovercourt
64. Christie Pits
65. Yonge & Elm to Yonge & Charles
66. St. George Station
67. York Blvd. to York Blvd.
68. Vine & Keele to Vine & Pacific
69. Jane & Dundas to Dundas & Royal York
70. Edna & Dorval to Dorval & Chelsea
71. Queen's Park
72. Glenlake & Keele to Glenlake & Pacific
73. Bathurst & Bloor to Bathurst & Dupont
74. Bloor & Brunswick to Brunswick & Harbord
75. Yonge & Isabella to Yonge & Wellesley
76. Dundas & Pacific to Dundas & Quebec
77. Dundas & Indian Grove to Dundas & Heintzman
78. Black Creek to 407
79. Bloor & Indian Grove to Indian Grove & Glen Gordon
80. College & Major to College & Spadina
81. Bloor & Christie to Bloor & Ossington
82. Dufferin & Bloor to Dufferin & Dundas
83. Dufferin & Bloor to Dufferin & Dupont
84. College & Shaw to College & Ossington
85. Keele & Bloor to Keele & Stockyards
86. Yorkdale Station
87. Dundas Square
88. Bloor & Yonge to Yonge & Charles
89. Spadina & Queen to Spadina & Dundas

90. Queen's Park
91. Annette & Evelyn to Annette & Quebec
92. Bloor & Bathurst to Bathurst & Ulster
93. Keele & Dundas to Dundas & Pacific
94. Queensway & McIntosh to Queensway & Royal York
95. Roncesvalles & Howard Park to Roncesvalles & Grenadier
96. Black Creek & Eglinton to Black Creek & Lawrence
97. Roncesvalles & Grenadier to Roncesvalles & Boustead
98. Christie Pits
99. Queen's Park to York Blvd.

# TAG & RUN

## CANTO ONE

**1.**

No! I am not Madame Cezanne
Nor was meant to be

Those wine bottles in your neighbour's garden
Have they begun to sprout?

The Art of Work in the Age
Of Mechanical Oppression

A future right turn
Overwhelm your comfort zone

A lyric in flight

**2.**

Reading Sherlock Holmes on my phone
Private i-policing

"Electricity comes from other planets"
Everyone suddenly discovering infrathin

Soprano season
The bald-headed convertible

Divers drivers
Sunburned quinquagenarian

Too angry for grammar

**3.**

Good things happen to bad people
Mark's metonymic moments

*Consider the* [sex life of the] *Lobster*
Peterson's Patreon

Gofuckme
Crowdsourcing corruption

Make art
Or cut the rope

Fill the lack with patriotic acts

**4.**

We turned the lights down low
& had a hookah on the patio

The nattering of matter
Curved heir ball

Herbed suburb
The scent of dryer sheets

Atomizes the atmosphere
Blue screen moon

Wild Posting! Rough Sleeping!

**5.**

No need for Polaroids anymore
Aloe dobro

Uh-oh Seven
A carjack rustler

Surfing bard
Wyrd is the word

Paper view, box sheets
Scandal tables

Don't let the barstools grind you down

**6.**

Nothing's normal
Nibiru rendezvous

An autumn inferno
Dante's détente

Taking a née
Invest in oxygen

"Suffocation time"
Grievable debts

Phish & cut vape

**7.**

A glabrous given
To argue the guru

Don't be a poet at the picnic
Proletarian laughter

Relentless raccoons
Simian imperialism

Churches convert into condos
In a town without irony

Unsent by the Sender

**8.**

Days like these it's
Easy to imagine the end

Asphalt around a tree
The work of a knucklehead

Dude with a Doberman
A hazmat splash pad

Catastrophe actors
Hirohito mon amour

Never met an Ezra I liked

**9.**

Our Virgo viragos
Be there with belles on

The blues clues
A ploy & its fog

The problem with
Brunch at Tiffany's

Learning the dog's old tricks
Milking the dinosaur

To be cooler than capitalism

# CANTO TWO

## 1.

Chaucer the Robber
A rake among the leaves

Can't bear tales
#timesup timebombs

Ontario, Quebec, & Me
YYC makes three

Dada alleys
Conceptual allies

Catastrophe actors

## 2.

The eventual left
The glorious orange

Running to neutral
The keystone copes

Forest Hill Girls
Typical thrills

Caffeinated hummingbirds
People with glass tigers

Rock paper scission

## 3.

The Home of the Devils
"For all your lifestyle demands"

Which finder
In general?

Rude moon
How high the loons

Frog-marched or hog-tied
Crush poetics

As nude as the muse

**4.**

Back in the Dark Park
Undone by undines

Wax to win
The wizard of L'eggs

Walks & balks
Nag & shun

Air ere err
A thick wall, a short fence

How to do words with things

**5.**

Eternal witchcraft
Perpetual spells

Penetrating problems
Gap magic

Weak leak
Mourning sex

Antenna dilemma
Rude operator

A saucy grandma

**6.**

SJW swag
Virtue marketing

Signals sedition
Swamp draining slugfests

Jung's dummy
Faux *philosophe*

Lame lamentations
Of the moronic MRA

A punk punch at the patriarch

**7.**

Bozos & monotheism
A Freudian shit

Shake your money faker
Counter with fits

Floating like Lacan's tin can
*The French Reflection*

Nocturnal confessions
Whet dreams

Through the looking guise

**8.**

The Big Lib Ousting
Dudes defaming

Ordering *Orlando*
Pay vanity's fare

Binaries encoded
Bunyan's Bible

Pilgrims regress
Nationalist frogs leap back

Tense the season to be trolling

**9.**

Duncan's don'ts
Some Imagist ingredients

Endangered supplements
Vortical blinds

Rock drill mining
Diving for laurels

Fathers become führers
Second generation usury

Why the LANGUAGE poets voted for Reagan

# CANTO THREE

## 1.

Grim funk
Anansi antipathy

The sun shines cyan
Sky son scion

CC in CF
A socialist proposition

Punning on paternity
In perpetuity

Presumes a seagull

## 2.

iCloud wandering
Words worth nothing

The Boring Highways of Ontario
404 Not Found

Corpse paint
Night again

The hellmouths of bumpf
Evil revels

Make them eat gay cake

**3.**

Replacing every "the" with "die"
Pardon the gun

Like mangoes in PoCo
A taste invasion

Foucault ruins the party again
Shopping for gazed harm

A truffle pig
Take a cold power

"Drunk enough to say I love you"

**4.**

A Sober Man Looks at the Missile
The breach at Port Dover

Your daily horror scoop
The Gemini scheme

Depression in the blood
ATM taboo

Die & dry
Beckett's bile

As queer as Walt Whitman's beard

**5.**

A rude Buddha
Yoko's no-nos

The Wrath of Cons
Return of the red eyes

The white godless
Marking Graves

Ford of Misrule
Making the 'coke it

Douchebag dudes with drones

**6.**

Metro harlequin life
Joke's on TO

Petting another man's dog
Brawling's in, coming down

Being Houyhnhnm
Yahoo blues

An eye, climatized
Pander vision

Fight paths of the Empire

**7.**

Watch Holmes
Monitor Moriarty

A who Donne it
Watson second?

Abdominal Romeo
The broiling children at bicycle camp

The *Sun*'s stupor
Solar torpor

Moldy Peaches & Moody Beaches

**8.**

Canada Post-
Ashkenazi Anishinaabe

Two nations under clods
Anti-Semitism & assimilation

Fuck breathing fire
Spit sparks instead

Almost cut my fear
Flying my antifa flag

Smoke 'em when you see them

**9.**

Talkin' about fascists
Mobsters are real

NoMeansNo announce a reunion
The Durutti Column supporting

Teeth-grinding geopolitics
A recreational chew bone

A war of wine & oil
Apathetic Instagram audiences

Tranquilized bear falls from tree

# CANTO FOUR

**1.**

Do you remember,
Hüsker Dude

Two ninjas on a first date
Coy koi

Orientalism arises
The Said truth

Imaginary Icicle Works
Sharia Syria dissimulation

Innerburb scum of the earth

**2.**

Language is algae
Slippery signification

Green ideology
Sleeping furiously

Collarless rudders
Mewl Britannia

Brexit rules the raves
Applied Ballardism

*How to Read Donald Cuck*

**3.**

If the first tool was a weapon
Irony & whine

Bread & surfaces
Better than buck a beer

Let's get ready to crumble!
Cue the violence

A juice box hero
Stoned & dethroned

The sought weed factor

**4.**

Ever tinkering with chance
A triolet a day

Plus one for fuck
The nine muses who desert us

Nonnet's the game
Let's lay it bald

His or her graphic metafriction
Molson Lindy

The Canadian Postmortem

**5.**

Haussmann hits home
Mount Pleasant, not Paris

Instamatic Fields
Metric resistance

As arrogant as Aragon
Breton's braggadocio

Surrealism's cynosure
Steve's reprieve

That's when I preach to my evolvers

## 6.

Basket's drinking rhythm
Pauline's pearls

Mainlining quarters
An arcade choir

Scooby Doo dialogue
Heavy Metal kids

Red fronting
Running flared

The Man Who Taught His Asshole to Clap

**7.**

The Missing Licks
Gave me a dud bun

Tempting tows
Lines dawn

A Schmaltzrock sampler
Julian's deusuicide

God's firing squad
No place like om

Masturbating to your Namaste

## 8.

Soon Over Miami
Red State castaways

Senior defenestration
Pining for the Isle

Fidel's fallout
Cesaire's shakeup

A toasted tempest
Teapot dictation

Reading the leaves

**9.**

Crying on autopilot
Drone depression

Phantom flyovers
Ghost planes of golfers

The Gin Genie
Smashed Sufis

Rumi to roam
Pals of Stein

Make the word your salon

# CANTO FIVE

## 1.

A plant-based riot
Vegans revenge

Florid fauna
A free-range fraternity

Estrogen wonders
Porcine proclivities

O Brave Nude World
Belfies & butt facials

Got a hate sonnet with your name on it

**2.**

She returns to bed
Her underwear still wet

From backseat kneebucking
Inner thigh fingerbruises

At least learn a new trick
Share the filth

Plead the gift so as
Not to sublimate oneself

Brag on the stun all day

**3.**

Nine lines per diem
Or cocaine nights

Twice bitten while high
Tripped up kicks

The bores of perception
A peerless plowman

Codeword CoBrAs
Crossed Christs

In perpetual emotion

**4.**

Yammering managers
Dugout dictators

Springing for the six
Touch three

Balked in a run
*L'eau hazard*

Imagine Maxwell's scheming
Or sliver slammer

A paper lady or a painted tiger

**5.**

Flaming logos
In the beginning was the fraud

Only a sandbox castle
If the Six were mine

7 would be an L upside down
Your friendly neighbourhood legerdemain

Tyros of tyranny
Infant infantries

Bounty Bear (he's searching)

**6.**

A Kipling for every country
Diaspora is not the exception

The hypocrisy of herbivores
Monsanto insanity

Soy: "bomb"
Portnoy's confreres

Carnivores incarnate
Not to be a live/evil

But to keep evoloving

**7.**

The corvus chorus
A trio or twa

Panegyric & praise
Posey & buzzem

*A Dull's House*
Ibsen interminable

The ectoplasm of a flea
A puce phantom

Alas, poor York!

**8.**

My sassiest namesake
In a conspiracy of mirrors

Not raving but downing
Given name no claim to fame

Larkin's laments:
So much sex in the sixties

Or when jazz stopped being slavish
When you have everything you need

You start looking for things to want

## 9.

It's come to steal or steel
Forage or forge

No collusion—a witch hunt?
Fat cat rhymes with plutocrat

Swordwords
Plow the shareholders

Sow a road of bones
& capitalist corpses

To ignite the light

# CANTO SIX

## 1.

Psychopomp entelechy
Word-a-day wardens

Potential cues
In an Aristotelian crossword

Trollops or trolls
Toils of tenure

Fist world problems
Snake fight sinecure

Two guides to every glory

**2.**

*Odi et Amo*
A thousand misses

& add another score
When the pitcher leaves the mons

Venus ridiculous
Balls in, coming down

Warmed up & ready
Wreckers abound

Venomous to a fault

**3.**

Afrikaner argots
Living a zef life

Cousin to blackface
Wipe trash

Eighties' anxieties
Walls fall without recoil

Always remember
The fits of September

Never met a nice Republican

**4.**

Half through my life
Lost in a darkmode

Dante's depression
More damning than a détente

The circles of Indian Road
Grove, Crescent & Glen Gordon

 Freemen are a joke
(To say nothing of the dog)

Low, the leash-man

**5.**

To serve or save
Burden the net

Worth two in the push
Toward temerity

Folk tales of the reconnection
Thee blind vice

Carter carved it first
A bloody camber

Slouching toward bedlam

## 6.

He do the politesse
With different choices

Mole hole mimicry
Wishing for fishers

Railroaded by the man
Lizards spring

Claustrophobic as Kafka
Josephine the nine mouses sing

The harrowing of hello

## 7.

Beard burns
Bristle branding

Seared by the stripping
Weather reminders

Autotipsy
To reel with one's own eye

A cocaine socialist
Champagne campaigns

Petty on the inside

**8.**

Yabba dabba doobs
Barefoot sparks

Prehistoric combustion
Fossil fools

Light, sweet, rude
Girl mollies

Often oneiric
A creepy treehouse

Jesus waves

**9.**

Vegetables of distinction
Kitchen impediments

Gene spicing
Meme warfare

Phonephobia
Voice male

Milton mediates
A war haven

Let there be fights

# CANTO SEVEN

## 1.

The problem with trolleys
The Tragedy of the Commute

Toronto torsion
Mechanicals of the metropole

Bottom nature Snug starvelings
A scam in High Park

CNE skidaddler
A Lakeshore lockout

Deploy the summer

## 2.

The sadness of stockings
An uninked ankle

Solipsists wear shades
Sophists smear sunscreen

Dorsal diorama
Splayed & sprayed

All the pretty little divorces
The story of my strife

The timed healing of wounds

**3.**

Stopping in Scarborough
For slurpies & smokes

Wayne's Void
Karmic relief

Admired Mikita
Doughboys of Dnipro

In keeping aground
Not sleeping around

Ghosts in the *agora*

**4.**

Trains make plains
The National Scheme

A bookshelf, like whiskey
Straight or neat

Jersey barriers bar bombers
Uncanny valley

Helping hypocrites
To pull up their stocks

A tear gas awakening

**5.**

Unmanned by Friday
Cruised by Crusoe

No age of reason, in faith
Wretched at birth

Macho Modernism
Versus knockout Negritude

Maybe Digital Humanities could help
To read & disappear

A sentimental attachment to bookmarks

**6.**

Bashō's Ponge
Bucolic batrachians

Fired for breeches
Hot pant pedagogue

Dali's ants
Itchy palmistry

A numinous dog
Oppen's opprobrium

If Keele Street could speak

7.

New Mysterians
Questioning the mark

Zeno, not Solomon Kane
Come-on puns

Skeptical scop
Skalded by the vates

A midsummer's steam
The Globe's warning

Clinamen change

**8.**

Sucking the dregs
The lees of me

No jab too small
Under unrest

Moving the gaol posts
Blocking heaven's door

That hat's something I can't explain
Torpedo your libido

Better than the average bare

## 9.

Not smarter, I see
Endowed like a Ken doll

Punch drunk by the pounder
40 oozes a dram

Really up the function
The promoting of proles

Grounds for execution
The killing deals

One man's roar is another man's yielding

# CANTO EIGHT

**1.**

Renovicted by the removalists
Elect the preterite

The Anne brand
Pigtails over breadfruit

Oh, & fuck your airshow
& the Franklin Expedition too

You foul the sea
A view to an ill

Change is loosed

**2.**

Joy to the word
The bored have come

Readership as ridership
Transfer the tension

Lost in the transition
Last stop Union

Extreme junction
Appoint the sick

Needles & sins

**3.**

A stationary arc
Circle to Cockney

Dicky bird fish hook
Slang removes the tag

Composing in code
An ex mars the plot

A novel approach
A kiss from my prose

Ruins the ruse

**4.**

A Nile song
Denies annihilation

The Book of the Bed
Egyptian exogamy

Derrida's supplementary son
Rondo à la twerk

Nimrod's battle for Babel
All fall noun

Semantic scattering

**5.**

Never escape high school
A student council with something at stake

Reaching that stage (age)
Where if you die in the game

You die for real
Keeping sheep by moonlight

Eve's apple cedes
Presidential pets

A careless cat

**6.**

TED talks
Bears picnicking

A big surmise
Obvious outcomes

No notes connotes
Serious scholarship

Slippery citations
An elusive eel

More to say about mores

**7.**

Know you're a product
Saints align

Debord Boyer Cesaire & Smith
Poets & performers turn tropes

Too old to pen odes
Cattle & Cain

The estrangest day
Lucifer Sam I Am

Another dick & his wall

## 8.

Not your dad's dope
Stronger by the generation

Opioid catachresis
There's evil in Cleveland

Bastard from a basket
Moses unmoored

Cleopatra's miscegenation
Caesarion or caesarian succession

Too many seizures are not good

## 9.

A specious fraternity
In the ploys of summer

Equivocal equipoise
The only Leafs that matter

Dominico divides a field
Where fascism was fought

The hug of thugs
Hooligan hospitality

Washed in the blood of the fans

# CANTO NINE

**1.**

To make it to forty-nine
Tuppence past the stretch

Keep pushing that dead car down the highway
& eventually you will arrive

& in the end it's only a koan
Which it is

To say you played the game well
But to leave nothing behind

It's rule for rats

**2.**

Delouse your guitar
Bosh! said rudely

Sing a song of nonsense
Now we are two score & eight

To reign a rainy kingdom
Smoke in the water

Banjo bards of the badlands
Why the jackass laughs

You're not the only hypocrite at the funeral

**3.**

A doubtful gust
Wind in the pillows

Drapes drift, queen-size quilts
Liminal rain refrain

"You kiss like a girl"
Bisexual conversion

A dukedom of looks
Thrown for a throne

A strange pair of dice

**4.**

Hideous organs
The music we fake

Three tramp theory
A Shropshire Dad

Alas, in blunderland
Through with the book bash

Launch season failure
How shall we sing with a strange band?

The way must be tired

**5.**

Believe in utter dogwash
Relatable mediums

What the lightening said
In *Finnegan's Wake*

Your breathe so bad
I can hardly breath

Begs the exception
With re-guards to re: Marx

Proves the rue

**6.**

When you *want* to like flamenco
Texas is the reason

Kahlo response
Diego skullduggery

My outrageous eyebrows
Hair apparent

Now books as burdens
Dancing with my shelves

What you can read before you die?

## 7.

& if I listen to Rush
& watch ballet, who shall not say

The harpy Genesis is in my stronghold
& that my amoeba is not amused

Punch the wall
Pasta marks the colander

Sisyphus situations
Shoulder to boulder

Must be imagined sappy

**8.**

The secret to wait loss
Everything that exists

Is here because someone
Before you built it

The manufacturing of landscapes
Utopia of unitary urbanism

So you stroll like a *homo sacer*
Baring & bearing life

The ignoble pursuit

**9.**

The loneliness of a long-distance writer
The skewbald letters

Guru Gormenghast
Drinks before you peak & speak

So we wine & scribe
Talk the walk

Scrawling the walls
An asemic signature

Tag & run

May 7 – September 8, 2018
Toronto

# Notes

*Walking & Stealing* is a long serial poem composed over the summer of 2017. Each section was composed at a park in Toronto & the GTA between innings of games in which my son, a Peewee AA ballplayer, was pitching & fielding. The composition time of each section is the length of a game, & the first draft of each section was recorded in a notebook in the shape & design of a baseball. While the impetus & origin of the poem is juvenile sports, baseball is not so much the subject of the poem, but the site & event that allows the poem to arise as I explore duration, association, & subjectivity. The game of baseball also functions as an analogue for poetic exploration; for example, the title of the poem refers to plays in baseball (two ways in which one can gain a base without hitting a ball), but also to psychogeographic perambulation & "stealing" as poetic intertextuality.

*Intentional Walks* draws its title from a problematic baseball strategy, but the poem itself is more interested in thinking & composition while walking (gesturing to Aristotle's peripatetic school or Lyceum). Each of the 99 poems was composed during a predetermined walk ("intense" walks, or walks "in tension") with the resulting poems sometimes being rather long, & others being a single line, perhaps reflecting the lack of ambience found on these streets, or else the walker's disengaged mental state.

*Tag & Run,* in keeping with baseball's "magic number nine," consists of nine cantos, each canto containing nine poems, each of which are nine-line poems. The title started as a baseball term, but then also came to refer to the game of tag: textually "tagging" a reference & then "running" with what associations it leads to. Then, by the end, I realized that it was also a metaphor for this type of writing itself: tagging as graffiti & the relinquishment of authorship (to run away) that occurs in a (Spicer-inspired) serial poem. Make a sign & deny it. Marks of spectres.

## Acknowledgements

This book is for Cy Cain, a boy of summer, the reason that this book exists, & someone I learn from—& am inspired by—every day.

If the book has a co-dedicatee, it is Tim Conley, who convinced me that this project was viable as a stand-alone composition, & who also curated *Marks of Cain*, a beautiful poetic album for my 50th birthday, just as these poems were being completed.

Dani Spinosa, editrix extraordinaire! A killer eye & ear, who always gets my music references & puns.

Andy Weaver, fellow struggler, for commiseration of all kinds, & for comments on drafts of the manuscript.

Thanks to Sharon Harris for the cover & author photos.

rob mclennan published sections of this as an above/ground chapbook (*Tag & Run: Canto One*) & in *Touch the Donkey*. He also happens to be an upstanding gentlemen who sustains writing communities in Canada & abroad.

A great citizen, critic, & poet (who wishes to remain anonymous) published sections of this book through Happy Monks Press, as did Adam Katz in *Partial Zine*.

Many thanks to Jay, Hazel, & Reid Millar, the Book*hug family, who make wonderful things happen & who are both personal friends & friends to literature in this country.

A tip of the hat to those who lend both overt & implicit support: Jonathan Ball, Doug Barbour, derek beaulieu, Greg Betts, Lily Cho, Adam Dickinson, Ray Ellenwood, Beatriz Hausner, Peter Jaeger, Alex Porco, Art Redding, Eric Schmaltz, Kate Siklosi, Jason Wiens, & Suzanne Zelazo.

Photo: Sharon Harris

## About the Author

Stephen Cain is the author of six full-length collections of poetry and a dozen chapbooks, including *False Friends*, *I Can Say Interpellation*, *Zoom*, *Etc Phrases*, *American Standard/Canada Dry*, *Torontology*, and *dyslexicon*. His academic publications include *The Encyclopedia of Fictional and Fantastic Languages* (co-written with Tim Conley) and a critical edition of bpNichol's early long poems: *bp: beginnings*. He lives in Toronto where he teaches avant-garde and Canadian literature at York University.

## COLOPHON

Manufactured as the first edition of
*Walking & Stealing*
in the fall of 2024 by Book*hug Press

Edited for the press by Dani Spinosa
Proofread by Shannon Wibbs
Design and typesetting by Gareth Lind, Lind Design
Typeset in Proxima Nova
Cover image by Sharon Harris

bookhugpress.ca